THE WHOLESALER'S COMPANION

SUCCESS HAS LITTLE TO DO WITH *WHO* YOU KNOW

CRAIG M. PORTER ROLLINS

ISBN: 1456492845

Printed in the United States of America

Illustration by Mark Jarman
Edited by Kimberly Rollins
Book design and layout by Paige Sauer

First Edition

www.AGoodI-Do.com
Twitter @AGoodIDo
Facebook "A Good I-Do"

Table of Contents

Introduction

The purpose of this book is to provide a simple, quick and easy reference for those who rely on sales to earn a living. The information contained within these pages is a culmination of years of personal and shared experiences from thousands of clients, customers and wholesalers. The majority of recent interviews have been primarily in the field of financial services; however the principles for success presented are universal and work across multiple industries.

I have kept this book short and to-the-point because I don't believe that reading volumes of pontificating drivel will help you any more than a few well-written and direct anecdotes that can be immediately applied. Successful people are doers – they conceive of a plan to move forward and launch into activity. If it doesn't work the first time around they simply adjust their plan and begin again.

This book is for those who want to launch into activity and have a dogged determination to achieve a goal.

There is no secret to success. The only difference between those who fail and those who succeed is how many times they get back up after being knocked down.

How to Read This Book

It is not necessary to read this book from front to back. It is written in sections, not chapters, which will provide you the opportunity to follow your own path. Pick a section and dig in. The right side of the pages have been marked so each section is easy to locate. I have always used quotes to help me stay focused on the things that I believed were most important, so I have included several in this book to help you. One last thing, you have my permission to highlight and mark this book up as much as you want. Enjoy!

Key Terms

Wholesaler and Sales Representative - are used interchangeably to identify a person who is employed by a company that makes or provides a product or service that is sold through a business, firm or retail outlet.

Company/Sponsor - are used to represent the company that provides raw material or manufactures, produces or provides the initial products or services (including financial instruments or materials) to the business, firm, manufacturer or retail outlet.

Client - represents the business, firm or retail outlet through which the manufactured product or service is provided to the public market. This would include: clothing stores, financial services firms, and manufacturing companies that purchase raw material through a sales representative. A wholesaler or sales rep is introducing products or services to these establishments in hopes of gaining additional outlets for their products. The client and the customer are not interchangeable and represent two very distinctive entities.

Customer - may represent the general public as the end user that purchases products or services from a business, firm or retail outlet or a manufacturer that purchases raw material. For the purposes of this book any entity that requires material, products or services for their own use is a customer.

"Nothing great was ever achieved without enthusiasm."

Ralph Waldo Emerson

ONE

TRUE SUCCESS STARTS WITH HOW YOU ARE KNOWN

When was the last time you were involved in a conversation and the topic turned to someone who recently jumped up in the corporate ranks? The subject of others' success is common coffee-break banter and can be both motivating and detrimental, depending on the overall tone of the participants.

I will freely admit that over the years I have been involved in one or two such conversations from the less-than-positive side. These conversations usually start with, "Did you hear who just got promoted? They were only given that position because they know ____." It is my intent to dispel this fallacy.

The Tale of Bob:

These stories are based on experiences with numerous real people. The names of all the characters in this story are fictitious and any similarity to any person living or deceased is coincidental.

Bob Baxter is a representative for Myriad Industries. He has worked in this particular sector for many years, and Myriad is the latest company that has employed him. Bob has great work experience and knows a great number of potential clients. Bob's sales performance is not very reflective of his tenure and professed connections.

To gain a better understanding of why Bob may be experiencing some difficulties, we need to hear from those who have worked with Bob over the years.

Geoffrey Tillston, Manager and potential client of Myriad products:

"I have known Bob since he was with Amtel Corp. He was just an assistant to the rep we dealt with and was okay to work with, but he was forgetful. On several occasions we had to resubmit orders. He was great at getting the items we needed overnighted to us, but it happened more than a few times every year. The guy we work with now confirms every order the next day and emails us when the shipment has left the warehouse. It has been a great experience."

"Bob would have to show me that his memory has greatly improved before I would consider changing to Myriad. It isn't that Myriad's products are bad or of less quality than what we are currently using. They're fine, but I can't deal with having to worry about whether or not our order is going to be delayed even one day with the current economic pressure."

Marjorie Peck, Controller, L&L Manufacturing, supplier to companies like Myriad and Amtel:

"Bob is a very nice man, and I would say he is an honest person. He does, however, have a bit of an obnoxious personality. I don't think he is intentionally overbearing, but he doesn't always know when the conversation is over. I would prefer to work with someone other than him when dealing with material-related orders."

W. Gunderson, Bob's last manager:

"I can tell you Bob is a great guy and isn't afraid of work. Bob's biggest obstacle with us was, well, Bob being Bob. He was always scrambling, trying to pick up pieces because he forgot to write things down. He would repeatedly call some of his clients to make sales, forgetting that they had already purchased. He was a little too aggressive at conferences, and we noticed that many of our better customers assigned to Bob started asking to be reassigned to other reps."

"Bob's performance got worse and worse as he tried to overcome his poor performance. He literally became even more in-your-face with follow-up and sales calls once his performance numbers continued to drop over a six-month period. He was in a downward spiral, even after we talked to him about letting up a bit and trying service calls for a while. He couldn't just relax and let the client talk. It was always push, push, push and all he ended up doing was pushing away his current clients and prospects."

"It takes 20 years to build a reputation and five minutes to ruin it. If you think about that, you will do things differently."

Warren Buffett

"There aren't many of our current reps who have Bob's experience or technical expertise, but I couldn't keep Bob around because he couldn't back off fourth gear. When he left, I gave him a letter of recommendation and I hope he lands at a company that can take advantage of his experience, but I wouldn't put Bob in front of a client — not unless he can throttle back or take a conversation skills course."

Here we have a classic example of someone who is very much in-the-know of the right people. Bob has years of experience, is considered to be knowledgeable by current and former employers, and likely has a contact list developed over years of sales calls and conferences.

Based on the aforementioned argument that someone is successful simply because they know the right person doesn't hold up to scrutiny. I propose that we correctly redefine the "who you know" terminology to the following:

It isn't who you know that makes one a success, but rather how you are known by the right people in key positions that creates opportunities for success. How you are known is more important than who you know.

You might know someone very powerful, like a local politician, CEO or a multimillionaire. You may be fortunate enough to know a national celebrity or world renowned sports figure, but if they know you as anything other than a phenomenal person with great integrity, foresight, knowledge and a get-it-done attitude, what good does it do you? None. No good comes from this knowledge. In fact, it will likely hurt you if you are known in any of the following ways: lazy, dishonest, untrustworthy, unknowledgeable, me-first attitude or just someone who is always chasing that big deal but never sees anything through.

How much opportunity would you really get from any of the people you know simply by knowing them? The answer is obvious and probably not that surprising. You will get no opportunities from people that know you in a negative way.

Your future depends on how you conduct your life every single day. Some things can be overcome with time and a change in behavior, but that may not guarantee that you will be given another chance. Who would trust Bernie (the billion dollar fraudster) with their life savings if he were to suddenly be released from prison on good behavior?

Your opportunities for success in business, family and life in general aren't based on who you know, but how you are known by those who can give you an opportunity to succeed. The following examples will help you get a feel for how being known can and will have an impact on your opportunities for success.

Mr. Smooth Operator:

I think this description says it all. Mr. Smooth Operator looked as if he had just stepped out of a bad "B" movie. He had the gelled hair, the gold chains, fancy suit and spent most of the meeting talking about his boat and weekend parties. Though he appeared to be successful, and his time in the industry would reflect his knowledge and experience, his projected persona made it difficult to get past and understand the product being offered. Needless to say, he didn't get our business.

Disappearing Debbie:

One of the more frequent issues brought up in interviews and feedback received from clients was the non-returned email or phone call. In many cases, it was the amount of time it took for their wholesaler, sales rep or customer service person to get back to them. After the second day of no response, it appeared that their rep was either gone on vacation or they had left the company altogether.

Unfortunately, in the case of Disappearing Debbie, it was neither. It was just very poor follow-up skills and a lack of understanding that more than one day without returning an email or phone call is too long to wait. If you don't have time for a lengthy discussion or if you will be gone for an extended period without access to some form of communication, just let your internal counterpart know, or communicate it with a voice message on your phone. Utilize the "Out-of-Office" function in your email to inform clients of the time you will be unavailable with an option of another contact if it is urgent.

If you are difficult to contact or non-responsive to client calls and inquiries, the next thing that might disappear is your employment.

Type "A" Terry:

Terry is another really great person and sales rep. He is very experienced and has a great understanding of his product and company, and is a tremendous potential asset. Overall, I would consider this type of a wholesaler very successful. I love their enthusiasm and have enjoyed working with them over the years.

Terry's only drawback or weakness is that he must get through a predetermined sales presentation during his visit. It is somehow programmed into his DNA. He will find a way to manipulate the conversation to include the latest brochure or marketing piece to summarize the reason for the visit.

Though this may be a necessity for him, it can detract from something more important that could be occurring — the development of a relationship with his client. Doing business is the reason the wholesaler is there, but developing a relationship based on mutual respect and doing things the right way will be the reason many clients will become loyal to you and your company for many years.

Use common sense. If the intent of your sales call is to update and introduce new material then make that known, but don't mislead your client with a "social call" only to wrap up with a sales pitch.

"The reward for work well done is the opportunity to do more."

Jonas Salk

To this point, you have read mainly about those in the wholesaling business that have done things in a way that is detrimental to their success.

The following is a positive story about a wholesaler I know and have worked with for a number of years. He is no longer in the wholesale game, but his example is worth sharing. This is a great example of how you are known creating success.

Again, it isn't who you know that will bring you success; it is how you are known.

The Bulldog:

Bulldogs are great animals. They are protective, extremely loyal and when they decide to bite on something it's nearly impossible to get them to let go, and I should also mention they can be very stubborn. The following example is from my experience with a particular wholesaler I have dubbed "The Bulldog."

The nickname is meant in the kindest of terms and is very accurate in describing the person in the example that follows.

Charles had been a wholesaling rep for a number of years, and had called on my firm for almost three years prior to us ever placing any business with him. Where many would have eventually given up and stopped calling, this seemed to have little deterring effect on Charles. He continued to drop emails about different products or offerings as they came up several times a year. We would get a note or call about him being in the area and wondering if it was okay to come by to schedule a visit. As we worked in the same industry, our paths would cross at different industry conferences or conventions, and he was always quick with a smile and made everyone he met feel accepted.

I can't ever recall Charles not being fully engaged in a conversation with anyone during those conferences. If I didn't know better I would say he was conversing with close friends. That is just the way Charles is, and everyone who knows him will say the same.

As I mentioned, it took Charles quite a while to earn my business. I made the decision early in my career to thoroughly review every possible product and take at least one full year after being introduced to a new company before committing any funds. Most wholesalers don't particularly like my method for the simple fact that they don't immediately benefit from my acquaintance. Many wholesalers don't stay with their current employer that long and see my firm as too large of a time commitment.

Not so for Charles. For three years, he continued to keep in contact with us and was always friendly and courteous. He would bring different products by and make the presentation hoping that today would be the day he won our account. Each time he left empty-handed, but you wouldn't know that by his demeanor. He smiled, thanked me for my time and continued about his day.

That always left a great impression and made me determined to commit to doing business with him as soon as the right product came along. Charles had earned my business and hadn't sold a thing. When the day finally came and I said "yes" to Charles, he was almost in a state of shock. But true to what I had come to know about the man, he was great at following up and making sure that we had everything we needed to service our customers. If ever we had a problem, he was the first to get back to me and provided as many email updates as I needed. He was known for his great attitude and thoroughness.

When he left, his replacement had many of the same qualities Charles exhibited, and we continue our relationship with the company to this day. Now you can see why I dubbed him "The Bulldog." He remains a good friend and colleague and I don't ever see that changing.

How you are known by those in authority or key positions is important to your future opportunities for success.

TWO

STOP THE INSANITY AND GET OUT OF YOUR OWN WAY!

The example you are about to read is a culmination of both my personal sales experiences and those shared with me by sales professionals over the years. The main character, Alison, tries to change the outcome of her first experience as a wholesaler by doing the same thing over and over again expecting a different result — a commonly recognized definition of insanity.

Alison was fresh out of sales training. She had done very well on her product knowledge review and was excited to be assigned to her new area. Upon arriving, Alison's first responsibility was to establish a base of operations. The company had provided her a small budget and specific directions on the best locations for an office. She found a reasonable space and set up shop.

The next morning, Alison, armed with material and a list of possible prospects, marched out into her area looking for success. By 5:00 p.m. of her first day, she sat in her office, feet aching and worn out from a day of rejection. Not only had she not made a sale, she hadn't even gotten past the entire product introduction she learned in training. Resolved not to give up, she chalked up the first day to what the trainer called the "day of disappointment."

Alison regrouped, read through the product manuals and sales tips that the company had spent thousands of dollars and years of experience on, and retired for the evening. Over the next week Alison's routine was frustratingly similar. Each morning with a self-affirming pep-talk, a deep breath and smile on her face, she launched into professional salesperson mode, only to return to her office each night, feet aching, dishevelled appearance and no success.

She would look over the training manuals every evening, reciting over and over again the "proven techniques" outlined by her instructor. She would list every option and benefit her company's product could provide, but every day the result was the same — no sales and a dejected Alison. Something needed to change, and Alison was beginning to think she wasn't cut out for this career.

"Nothing will work

unless you do."

John Wooden

The next morning, Alison went through her morning routine of getting ready for a day of utter rejection. As she walked out the front door of her office, she bumped into Mr. Johnson. Mr. Johnson owned the gift and sundries store next to Alison's office. Mr. Johnson had lived and worked in this area all of his life, and was always willing to engage Alison in conversation when she stopped by his store or they bumped into each other as they came and went each day.

Alison's face must have given away her frustration as she and Mr. Johnson traded greetings this particular morning. "Why the long face?" asked Mr. Johnson. Alison fought back a wave of emotion and felt herself starting to tear up. Swallowing hard and biting the inside of her lip, she quickly composed herself and said, "I just can't seem to get past 'Hello' with the people in this area. If I don't start closing some sales soon, the company is going to reassign me, or worse, let me go. I'm trying everything I know and I just can't get people to see how great this product is. What am I going to do?"

Mr. Johnson, sensing that before him was a person in distress, said to Alison, "Would you like a cup of coffee? I'm on my way across the street to grab a cup. Why don't you join me and we can chat a bit about your troubles." Alison answered, "Thank you Mr. Johnson. That would be nice." "Call me Dan," he replied. Relieved to postpone what she expected to be another day of rejection and failure, they walked across the street to the café.

Over the next hour, Dan listened to Alison describe her experience with the sales calls she had made during the past month. He sipped his coffee and thoughtfully engaged her as she went on about her product and training. When she finished, Dan asked her a few questions about her decision to go into this line of work, to which she enthusiastically replied she loved the profession and couldn't imagine doing anything else, but couldn't have thought it would be this difficult.

Exasperated but grateful for the opportunity to unload her frustration, she asked Mr. Johnson for his advice on how to reach the people of his community. Dan asked Alison to tell him about the last few people she had called upon. Alison recited the conversations and ended each contact with the same conclusion, "Thank you, but we aren't interested." Dan then replied, "You didn't answer my question. I asked you to tell me about the people, not the exchange they had with you."

Alison stopped and thought for a moment, and then she told him their names and where they worked. Dan again responded that she hadn't told him anything about the people. He went on to share with Alison something personal about each of the people she had mentioned, stopping from time to time to ask if she was aware of certain titbits of information. Her reply was always the same, "No, I didn't know that!"

Then Dan said, "Let me share with you what I know of you." He proceeded to share all that he knew about Alison. Her surprise was evident by her expression.

"Life is relationships,
the rest is just details."

Gary Smalley

She didn't even remember sharing some of the things that Dan was able to recall. When he had finished, he said, "I'm going to put you in an uncomfortable position, Alison. I want you to tell me something that you know about me now."

Alison looked a bit stunned, and after hemming and hawing, she divulged very little information about Dan, sticking to basics, such as he owned the sundries store, was married (which she knew only because Mrs. Johnson had brought a welcome basket by when she first moved in) and that he had grown up in the area.

Alison could feel a flush of embarrassment rush over her face. She had been in this community for over a month and didn't know anything about the town, the history or even the next door neighbor that had always been friendly and helpful.

Dan invited Alison to dinner with him and Mrs. Johnson that evening. Alison happily agreed and spent that evening and the next several days getting re-educated on how to put relationships ahead of product.

Over the next several months, Alison applied all that Mr. and Mrs. Johnson had shared with her about the area and, more importantly, the people living in it. Alison got more involved with her community. She carried a small note pad with her, in which she would record interesting facts and personal notes about the people she met. She discovered the rich history and a wealth of information about the area and people who she had not seen or even known existed all around her.

Before she knew it, Alison was closing business. She was busier than she alone could handle and had to bring on an assistant. Her success had been noticed not only by her supervisor, but his boss the Managing Director of Sales and Marketing.

After only one year in her area Alison was setting a new standard for sales out of the Central District.

So impressed by her success, the Managing Director contacted Alison and asked her if she would write a report on her success and what she was doing to accomplish the tremendous sales numbers she was achieving. Alison was excited to tell of how she had achieved the success after struggling for the first few months. She completed a two-page summary of her experience and emailed it off to the director.

After receiving the report, the director brought it to the attention of the company president. They reviewed and discussed Alison's sales statistics with her immediate supervisor, then the president asked that a copy of Alison's letter be sent to every person on the sales staff. Alison received a congratulatory letter, certificate of appreciation and, more importantly, a raise for her efforts and resolve to overcome and simply get out of her own way.

The letter was sent to the entire sales staff, accompanied by a letter from the president saying that every member of the sales organization should immediately implement the ideas Alison had shared.

A senior sales rep in a neighboring area received the letter and after reading it, scoffed at the simplicity of the information contained within. That evening, he wrote a response to the Managing Director outlining all of the reasons that Alison's ideas would not work in his area or with the people that he had to deal with. His response was almost double the pages of Alison's original report.

This senior sales rep's response to a proven method is a great example of someone going out of their way to hold themselves back from success. Too often we allow our own preconceived ideas to stop us from reaching our potential. Successful people are not always smarter or better prepared. In many cases they are the ones who have the ability to step over the stumbling blocks they place in front of themselves and simply get out of their own way!

"A pessimist sees the difficulty in every opportunity; an optimist sees the opportunity in every difficulty."

Winston Churchill

THREE

CORE WHOLESALER KNOWLEDGE

Know Your Company's Story

This may seem basic and unimportant, but understanding your company's story, its beginnings and the "why" behind how your company came into being and why it is still around is vital to your understanding about the purpose of you doing your job and building your career. Does the company's mission statement or purpose resonate with you?

Even if your current employer is just a stepping stone to future opportunities, you need to be able to tell their company's story. It will have an impact on your ability to share your "why" about your position and your career choice with current and prospective clients. It is also necessary if you ever want to start your own business. If you can clearly and enthusiastically share your company's story it will be easier to develop and share your own story.

Know Your Product

If you are going to present a product or service, you need to understand as much as possible. Even cutting-edge products/services have a history. Find it, learn it and be able to share it with others. My experience has shown me that learning a product's history lends itself to humanizing the sales process. People have differences of opinion, but people are generally more alike than we want to admit. We all love a great story, and most of the world's great salespeople are great storytellers. Educate yourself on the product specifications, but don't forget the history behind the product as well.

Know the Client

In this day and age, there is no reason to not have some basic information about current and prospective clients in your product demographic. A simple search on any number of internet search engines should provide some information about the client personally or the company he or she works for.

If your search doesn't turn up what you would like to know, I suggest you start your initial meeting with a simple "get to know you" conversation.

I grew up in the south and had the great opportunity to watch my grandmother, a consummate businesswoman, find out everything she needed to know about someone she was thinking about doing business with over a 15 to 30 minute casual conversation.

One of my professors in college also gave me some great advice. He said that you can tell a lot about someone just by looking at what they have displayed in their office. Fishermen always have fish paraphernalia, golfers will have golf stuff. You will typically see photos of vacations, family, awards and certifications. People surround themselves with the things that make them feel good about who they are or remind them of happy moments in their lives. If you don't believe me, look around your own office. What do you like to surround yourself with?

People are busy and you need to be cognizant of their time; but ask yourself, "How many clients will I get if I rush through a sales presentation, literally throwing up every statistic and rehearsed product specification and never giving my intended client a chance to speak? Have I ever gotten a client this way? Have I ever bought a service or product from someone that talked at me and not with me?"

Take a deep breath and get to know the people you want to do business with. One of two things will likely happen. Either they will allow you more time to present your product/service, or you will determine that they may not currently be a good fit for your product/service. But, they may be more inclined to suggest someone who may be.

The outcome of this type of approach is the beginnings of respect for each other. You will have set a positive cycle in motion. As a sales rep or wholesaler, it is difficult to walk away from any meeting not achieving your end goal (a sale), but setting positive cycles in motion will ultimately result in many sales that will begin to appear like magic.

Persistence and patience, with a constant effort towards focusing on your client's needs, will pay dividends for many years.

Know Your Product's Target Audience

Who is the end-user of your product or service? Are there any common aspects within the demographics? Do they work or live in a specific area? Serve a niche market? Make more or less than a set income? Belong to a club, association, or professional organization? What is their educational background? Is the business seasonal? Are they a company or an individual? If they are an individual are they single, married, divorced, male, female, young, middle aged, retired, etc...?

Every product or service has a set demographic that is being targeted. The more you understand the end user of your product or service the better equipped you will be to provide value to the client. It will also serve in helping you spend more time with the most appropriate clients.

"Your ability to learn faster than your competition is your only sustainable competitive advantage."

Arie de Geus

You add value to clients by understanding who the ultimate user of your product or service is. Then, it becomes a matter of pointing your client in the right direction if they don't know where to look already.

WIIFT

Anyone who has had any type of sales training can tell you the meaning of WIIFM, "What's in it for me?" However, truly successful sales reps spend more time on finding the purpose and fit between their service or product and the prospective customer, or WIIFT, "What's in it for them?" I realize the acronym "WIIFM" is intended to help focus on the client or customers asking "What's in it for me", but saying "them" instead of "me" places the focus more outward.

Instead of focusing on what's in it for me, start focusing on the benefit to the client and see if their perception of you as just another salesperson changes to you becoming a trusted and knowledgeable asset to their business.

Presentation

Work on presentation skills, be informative and entertaining.

Everywhere possible, build on your clients' education and understanding of your service/product — don't make them drink from a fire hydrant if all they require is a sip now and again.

Be prepared to present to clients on a moment's notice. Have several quick and fast anecdotes ready to simply explain the four necessities of your program, WIIFT.

1. What is your product?
2. Who can benefit from it?
3. Why do you believe in it?
4. How can they get involved if they and their advisor can determine a fit?

Understand that some clients may not want to be product innovators.

Remember that when a client allows you to present directly to their customers, from the time you are introduced forward, you are an extension of their staff and are not only representing your company's product, you are also representing the client's company as well.

Value

Visit with a purpose. Even a relationship-building visit has a purpose.

Really explore your clients' business model:

- Who is their core customer?
- What areas do they excel at and what areas are they lacking in?
- Where do the majority of their customers come from?
- How can you help them grow?

Good reps and wholesalers will keep detailed information about current and prospective clients.

Conduct client calls to update on new developments, both good and bad news! This was an area that was repeated by almost every client we interviewed. No one likes bad news, but it is more difficult to take when the media is the one to break the news. I know from personal experience that getting the bad news in advance of a media event helps in preparing your customers in a way most convenient and beneficial. In addition, a wholesaler is supposed to have a relationship with their clients, and that means in good and bad times.

Know the customers who have purchased before (at least most recent purchases, their names preferably, not just a dollar amount).

Create interdependent clients, become an extension of their marketing team, educate them on what similar clients are doing to attract and retain customers. This will make you helpful in good years and invaluable in difficult ones.

"Information is not knowledge."

Albert Einstein

FOUR

DO'S AND DON'TS FOR SALES PROFESSIONALS

Sales Professional DO's

Do know your company's story.

Do know your product in every possible way.

Do know your client.

Do know and understand the targeted customer.

Do continual work on your presentation skills and be both informative and entertaining.

Do build up your client in the eyes of their customers.

Do teach, train and educate your client about your company and products in appropriate amounts.

Do use the four key points of WIIFT in your presentations.

Do remember that you represent the client when presenting to their customers.

Do visit with a purpose and remember that social visits have a purpose.

Do take time to understand your client's business model and ideal customer.

Do keep detailed and up to date information on all current and prospective clients.

Do conduct customer calls.

Do share good and bad news as soon as available. The sooner you get potential bad news to your clients the better.

Do return emails and phone calls promptly (same day or next day if possible).

Do communicate with clients and have alternative contact people available if you plan to be gone for an extended period of time.

Do follow up with clients after a new customer purchases, referring to the new customer by name if available to you.

Do create clients who are interdependent on you and the expertise you bring to their business.

Do assist clients with market knowledge and the latest in product developments.

Sales Professional DON'Ts

Don't pop in to your client's place of business unannounced and expect them to drop what they are doing to make time for you. Recognize that everyone is busy. It shows a lack of respect to assume you are more important than their schedule.

Don't show up and throw up. If you have a scheduled appointment to discuss your product or service, take a deep breath before the meeting starts and be relaxed and deliberate in your presentation. Allow ample time for questions and small talk, if appropriate.

Don't assume that the client doesn't understand the basics of your product.

Don't bad-mouth other sponsors, programs or former employers' products (even if they really do suck).

FOUR

Don't fail to recognize that competitors may have good products and services too (no place for a mine only attitude). You can have strong opinions about the greatness of your company, product or service and you should express your loyalty in the most appropriate manner. That does not include tearing down others.

Don't assume that a good relationship with a client from a former employer will automatically equate to sales with your new employer's product.

Don't push the need for sales today.

Don't visit without knowing your purpose. There is always a purpose for a visit. Make sure at least one of you (wholesaler, or your internal staff) knows what that purpose is and that you are communicating it to each other and your clients.

Don't think that visits are only about making a product sale and not about helping build relationships or the client's business (WIIFT).

Don't share what successful clients are doing without their permission and especially not with clients in the same market or geographical area. This is a serious no-no.

Don't commit to financial assistance to sponsor an event for your client and not come through with the cash or goods. Always verify with your management (measure twice, cut once). It is easier to under promise and over perform than the other way around.

Don't use deceptive tactics to get through the client's gatekeeper. Respect their protocols. This is my biggest pet peeve, and offenders that try deceptive practices will get blacklisted from my firm, regardless of how good the company or product is.

Don't get too technical unless you're asked to or you are speaking to engineers. The average client is less interested in technical specifications and more interested in whether or not the product meets their customers' needs. Clients, and ultimately the customer, want to know that the sponsoring company will stand behind the product and that it will perform as advertised. There will be plenty of time for the technical discussion. This would be a great reason to schedule a follow up visit. Tell the story (WIIFT)!

Don't spoon-feed your clients. If you do you will end up with a very demanding toddler that can't or won't produce unless you are feeding them prospects. If the career you want is business development, then quit and go to work for the client building their business. Helping your clients find new avenues for customers that can use your product is advisable and potentially very profitable, but don't just hand over resources. Teach them how to acquire those resources on their own. Teach them to be interdependent, not co-dependent. You need to be the resource, not the solution.

FIVE

BAD NEWS, YOUR MILLION DOLLARS IS GONE

There is never a right time to deliver bad news. In fact, I can honestly say I hate being the bearer of bad or difficult news and probably have the agreement of every sales or customer service-related person that this one thing is dreaded more than anything.

In several of the conversations and interviews many of the clients (advisors or retail businesses) stated their frustrations with their sales rep or wholesaler for not giving them less-than-positive news in advance of a media event, or worse prior to one of their customers bringing it to their attention. Bad news gets even worse if your customer is the one to inform you. No one likes to look stupid or uninformed to their customers. When this happens expect the fecal matter to roll uphill directly to the wholesaler or sales rep. All of this can be easily avoided with a quick phone call and some follow up about whatever situation is causing the bad news event.

I have had to deliver bad news to clients and customers at various times in my life. This particular event deserves to be told because of the sheer unbelievability of the circumstances and the ultimate outcome.

During the early economic crisis, I was working on finalizing the sale of a customer's business and subsequent purchase of another entity for their business portfolio. Everything was proceeding smoothly, the lawyers on both sides had agreed on the final details and monies had been placed in escrow at the chosen title and escrow company.

My client, Mr. Smith, and I had completed one transfer of funds to his new project and we were waiting on the final contracts to be reviewed by the next project's attorney to transfer the remaining $1,000,000 out of the escrow account to purchase the last piece.

It was late on Friday and the attorney assigned to review final documents had gone home early feeling ill. I called Mr. Smith and explained that it appeared the transaction wouldn't be completed until first thing Monday morning. He thanked me for the update, we chatted and both looked forward to the following Monday.

Early Monday morning, I received a call from the escrow officer representing the sellers, letting me know that they had not been able to contact anyone at the escrow company that was holding the funds for my client. They relayed to me that they were being told to contact a law firm in New York. I said that I would call and see if I could determine what the hang-up was and would get back to them shortly.

I contacted the escrow officer that had been assigned to us and was met with the same information that the sellers had received. All inquiries were being forwarded to New York. By mid-morning the bad news hit the wire services — the title and escrow company had filed for bankruptcy protection over the weekend. I was in shock. One of the largest escrow companies in the country had not only closed its doors over the weekend, but froze all access to the segregated accounts they held.

FIVE

Over the next several hours the bad news just kept compounding on itself. After verifying and re-verifying that there were no options to gain access to the $1,000,000, I had to make a call to inform my client to tell him that his money was effectively gone. One could argue that it wasn't my responsibility to call my client. I had not chosen the escrow company, could not be held liable or responsible for the escrow company's failure, and it would be easy to allow any number of other sources to inform my client, Mr. Smith, of his misfortune. I could even play dumb when he brought the news to me about the lost monies, vowing to assist him in every way possible.

Situations like this provide us with opportunities to make choices about who we are as professionals. We can choose to take responsibility or we can choose to take the path of least resistance. The latter is the default option, life will choose for us. The first is tough and usually requires great effort and is most often the better option.

I chose to take responsibility and make the call. Over my career I have discovered that simple truths are everywhere if we but choose to recognize them. Successful people understand the difference

"The price of greatness
is responsibility."

Winston Churchill

between simply accepting responsibility and taking responsibility. One is reactive, the other active. He, my client, might decide to shoot the messenger; I might lose him as a client or worse. As Mr. Smith's advisor it was my responsibility to keep him informed and educated on his options or lack thereof. I decided that as I had first-hand knowledge of the situation I must inform him as soon as possible.

How do you tell someone they just lost a million bucks? I took a deep breath and dialed my client's phone number. In a few seconds I was going to find out how to share this horrendous news.

The phone rang a few times and I heard the familiar sound of a digital click as the receiver connected the two lines. "Hello Mr. Smith. It's Craig. I have some bad news about your escrow account." "What's going on?" Mr. Smith replied. "It appears that the escrow company holding your funds filed for bankruptcy over the weekend and after verifying several sources, including the law firm representing them, your account is no longer accessible."

Silence, for what seemed an interminable amount of time followed. Then, Mr. Smith responded, "Are you kidding?" I can't remember the exact exchange after that, but Mr. Smith was suffering from the same initial shock I had experienced earlier that day. I continued to purvey the news in great detail. We discussed possible options and resolved to talk the next day after gathering additional information about this frustrating event. At the end of our conversation, I explained in the best possible way one can under this circumstance, how sorry I was to have to bring this news to him. But, I felt it was my responsibility as his advisor to be the one to inform him, even if it meant he might shoot the messenger.

He quietly thanked me for my efforts on his behalf and hung up. I am not sure how much time elapsed after the call was finished, but I remember feeling absolutely sick. I kept going over every shred of information, and tried to determine if there was any way possible this was a mistake and tried to determine a solution to get his money back.

FIVE

The story does have a reasonably good ending. With the help of a great law firm, we worked out a deal to get the majority of Mr. Smith's funds out of bankruptcy and even completed the original transaction. As of the printing of this book and to my knowledge, there have only been two entities that have successfully extricated their accounts from this bankruptcy with most of their funds intact. I am pleased to announce that Mr. Smith is one of the two. He continues to be both a client and friend.

You cannot be afraid of being the bearer of bad news. You may not always get the outcome you desire, but by not communicating bad news to your client or customers, I can almost guarantee that your relationship with them will be negatively impacted, if it continues at all.

SIX

SELF-ASSESSMENT

Developed especially for <u>The Wholesaler's Companion</u> by Dawna J. Grigsby Ed.S, L.P.C. Visit her page, *Zest of Life*, on Facebook.

The Sales Style Survey attempts to quickly measure client-centered tendencies through a self-report tool which may provide users with an effective measure of professional service orientation and hopefully will create some meaningful self-awareness.

SIX

The Sales Style Scale

This self-report scale is designed to provide information about the way you present yourself as a sales professional. Visualize yourself in your sales work as you work with clients and potential clients. Please respond to each question by using a number from the following key:

1 = Not like me
2 = Somewhat like me
3 = Like me

Part A

___ 1. When taking a self-assessment survey do you answer the questions in a way that makes you feel better about yourself?

___ 2. Do you lead your presentation with pay-out information hoping the client will focus on personal financial gain versus asking product/service-specific questions?

SIX

___ 3. Do you promote potential rewards or earnings to the client above focusing on the benefits to their customers?

___ 4. Do you stop by a client's office unannounced and request a meeting?

___ 5. Do you give some clients preferential treatment for personal reasons?

___ 6. Do you use hype to create client enthusiasm?

Part B

___ 7. Do you present technical specifications and potential benefits in a balanced presentation of your product/service?

___ 8. Do you take time to learn about your client before presenting your product/service?

___ 9. Do you schedule meetings with clients at least two weeks in advance?

___ 10. Do you gather information about the client's company prior to presenting your product/service?

___ 11. Do you ask for an explanation of each client's marketing approach?

___ 12. Do you know each client's target audience?

___ 13. Do you know how your product/service benefits various types of clients and/or customers?

___ 14. Do you easily acknowledge the limits of your product/service, when asked?

___ 15. Do you have confidence in your company and their product/service?

SIX

Scoring Key

Question number one is a paradoxical injunction used to help you care about being honest with yourself about the answers you choose. Part A requires a score reversal prior to adding the scores together. For the reversed questions, if you placed a #3 as an answer, change it to a #1 (all 1's become 3's, all 3's become 1's, 2's stay true).

Place the total here _____ (A).

Next, add up responses in part B. Place that number here _____ (B).

Add A_____ + B_____ = _____ .

Now, plot your score on the continuum below:

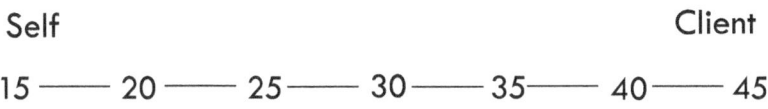

Where are you focused?

Self   Client

15 —— 20 —— 25 —— 30 —— 35 —— 40 —— 45

Use your score as an opportunity to assess your sales style and address your professional persona. How do you want to be known in your industry?

SIX

Summary

The brevity of this book is on purpose. It is intended to be a simple, easy and quick read so that you can immediately get to the doing part of being a wholesaler or sales rep.

Let's review key points to quickly and simply apply the concepts to real-world situations.

Concept 1:

It isn't who you know but how you are known by those in key positions that give you the greatest opportunity for success.

Notice that I didn't say you will be successful if the right people know who you are, only that you will be given an opportunity to be successful by those key people or those in authority depending on how they assess you as a person. Every day you should be working on improving your skills, being helpful to your colleagues and most importantly bringing value and useful help to your clients.

Concept 2:

Knowledge is a key component of your future opportunities.

The more you know about your company, product/ services, client, and ultimately the end user or customer, the greater your chances for success.

Concept 3:

Every industry has their own set of Do's and Don'ts.

Get familiar with the "Do's" in section four because they came directly from real clients. Ignore the "Don'ts" at your peril!

Concept 4:

Get out of your own way.

Don't overanalyze, don't get too technical, do listen, do get involved. Put the emphasis on understanding your clients, their needs, and their customers. Build relationships based on bringing the right products or services to the discussion, and remember that doing business isn't just about signing the deal. It is always about the people and relationships!

Concept 5:

Regardless of what your product or service is, you need to keep your presentation simple, easy to understand and easy for your client to apply when discussing it with their customers.

What does your product do?
Who can benefit from it?
Why do you believe in it?
How can customers get it if it is right for them?

Concept 6:

Bring something of value, but it doesn't have to be attached to your product or service.

Every visit doesn't need to be a sales call. You will learn more about your client in casual non-business settings.

Concept 7:

Good news, bad news, or just visiting to strengthen the relationship, remember to communicate, communicate and communicate even more when there appears to be unrest or confusion within your industry.

I will make you this promise, if you follow the basic principles outlined in this book one of two things will happen. Firstly, you will determine whether or not this career choice is right for you, or secondly, you will become as successful as you choose to be.
This isn't rocket science — it's human nature.

An Open Invitation

Over 25 years ago I began a journey to become more in-tune with my chosen career path. That path has led me to my current station in life, one that I enjoy and have many people to thank for helping me along the way. The research that contributed to my personal successes and to this book are ongoing and necessary.

I would like to invite all who read this book or hear me speak to share their sales experiences, both positive and negative, and help in the improvement of this profession. Only through shared experiences and monitored performance can we expect to reach our potential.

Email your experiences, thoughts and comments to Craig@AGoodI-Do.com or visit my Facebook page at *A Good I-Do.*

By emailing your experiences, thoughts and comments to A Good I-Do you are granting permission for your information to be included in ongoing research and future materials that may be published, used in training presentations, or speaking engagements.

*"There are no traffic
jams on the road to
the extra mile."*

Unknown

www.ingramcontent.com/pod-product-compliance
Lightning Source LLC
Chambersburg PA
CBHW071235170526
45165CB00003B/1106